D0433687

NOT
MANY
DEAD

NOT MANY DEAD

SENSATIONAL, SIZZLING
AND SOARAWAY PIECES OF
NON-NEWS

First published 2006 by
Aurum Press Ltd
25 Bedford Avenue
London WC1B 3AT
www.aurumpress.co.uk

Introduction copyright © 2006 by Nick Parker

Copyright © 2006 by Oldie Publications Ltd

The right of Oldie Publications to be identified as the author of this work
has been asserted in accordance with the Copyright, Designs and Patents
Act 1988.

A catalogue record for this book is available from the British Library.

ISBN-10 1 84513 197 5
ISBN-13 978 1 84513 197 5

10 9 8 7 6 5 4 3 2 1
2010 2009 2008 2007 2006

Designed and typeset in Garamond and Trade Gothic by
bluegumdesigners.com

Printed and bound in Great Britain by MPG Books, Bodmin, Cornwall

Contents

NOT
MANY
DEAD

Introduction

A FIELD GUIDE TO BORING STORIES

FOR SEVERAL YEARS now *The Oldie* magazine has been collecting examples of sensational, sizzling and soaraway pieces of non-news in its monthly 'Not Many Dead' column. The name refers to a headline with which the journalist Claud Cockburn claimed to have won a competition to get the dullest headline printed in *The Times*: '**SMALL EARTHQUAKE IN CHILE. NOT MANY DEAD.**' Some people with too much time on their hands say that they have checked, and can't find any record of the story actually appearing. No matter. In 2001, life imitated art when the Spanish newspaper *El Pais* ran the headline: '**VOLCANO ERUPTION IN MEXICO LEAVES NO VICTIMS.**' Splendid.

Connoisseurs of the boring story will recognise within this book its various sub-species: The most common – or *fatuous vulgaris* – is surely the 'famous person undertakes mundane task' story, a short item of news seemingly based on the belief that famous people inhabit a higher plane of existence than us mere mortals, and that any instance of them using a cashpoint or buying a packet of mints should be recorded as the Greek poets recorded the movements of the gods. These types of boring story are closely related to another type, *obvious drivellus* – news stories in which famous people treat the mundane details of their own lives as inherently newsworthy (Anne Robinson – I'm sorry that your dog died, I really am, but is the front page of the *Daily Telegraph* really the place to be wittering on about it?).

A growth area in recent years has been *tedious statisticus*, or 'self-serving survey', in which a company releases the results of a self-commissioned study proving whatever is most advantageous to themselves. A good example is: **'Women who spend the most time doing household chores have the highest sex drive.'** The survey was commissioned by Minky, a manufacturer of domestic appliances. A slightly less coherent example is this survey carried out by Vileda, makers of the 'super mop': **'Almost one fifth of Devon women would prefer to cut their toenails than clean the house.'** Quite what they were trying to prove is anybody's guess. Just what newspapers are doing printing this vacuous self-serving guff as though it were news is a deeper mystery still.

I confess that by far my favourites are the boring local news items (*tedious provincialis*): packets of peanuts (salted and dry roasted) stolen; flowerpots slightly damaged; small fires that put themselves out. And yet, and yet, within them, all human life is contained. What tragedies, what tears, what dashed hopes, what letters-fired-off-to-local-papers-yet-ignored, what administrative failings, what breakdowns in communication, lie behind headlines such as '**FED-UP DINNER LADY QUITS**' or '**WOMAN, 79, HAS TO CUT VERGES**'...?

Nick Parker

We are always pleased to receive cuttings.

Send them to:

Not Many Dead
The Oldie magazine
65 Newman Street
London W1T 3EG

Or email:
notmanydead@theoldie.co.uk

Further examples can also be found at: www.notmanydead.com

Acknowledgements

Many thanks to all the readers of *The Oldie* magazine who have submitted cuttings over the years. Your keen sense of the fatuous, the boring, the marginal, the uneventful and the downright dull has made this book possible.

Particular thanks must go to Francis Harvey, who in a recent poll was voted the top supplier of self-serving surveys.

CELEBRITY
SHOCKERS

Like father, like mother, like son; Wayne Rooney bears a striking physical resemblance to his parents, Wayne Snr and Jeanette.

DAILY MAIL

Singer Billy Joel badly gashed his finger on the lid of a tin of beans he was opening for his dinner at home in Long Island.

DAILY MIRROR

Troubled TV star Michael Barrymore suffered more misfortune yesterday when he was pecked by a swan.

EASTERN DAILY PRESS

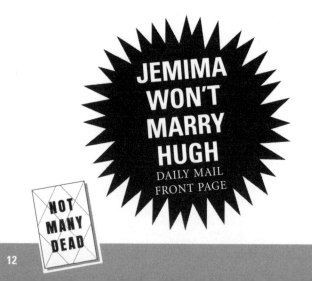

JEMIMA WON'T MARRY HUGH

DAILY MAIL FRONT PAGE

NOT MANY DEAD

Workmen dug up the drive of jailed author Jeffrey Archer's home in Grantchester, Cambs, to unblock a smelly drain.

SUN

* * * * *

Nigel Dempster, the *Daily Mail* gossip columnist, had a painful bruise after bumping his head on a door at his home.

DAILY TELEGRAPH

* * * * *

Wayne Rooney says he can't be bothered with lots of face creams. 'I just use soap, water and a razor.'

SUN

* * * * *

Actor Colin Farrell has a pair of lucky pants, worn on the first day of filming each of his movies. 'I've worn the same pair for about seven films now,' he says.

THE TIMES

* * * * *

Former *X-Files* star David Duchovny cannot wear his wedding ring because of an allergic reaction.

TV TIMES

The novelist Margaret Drabble tells readers of the *Sunday Times* that she has All-Bran for breakfast. Her husband, the biographer Michael Holroyd, 'prefers muesli'.

* * * * *

At a Chelsea cinema, Sandra and Michael Howard were debating whether to get Revels before wandering into the performance of *Mrs Henderson Presents*.

DAILY TELEGRAPH

Ladbrokes has cut its odds on Charlotte Church marrying Gavin Henson, the rugby international, from 5/1 to 3/1 after receiving up to 18 bets, mostly in the Cardiff area.

DAILY TELEGRAPH

* * * * *

According to Gwyneth Paltrow and Chris Martin, their daughter Apple, aged one, has started talking.

THE TIMES

Salman Rushdie has been spotted at Nice airport, revealed *Observer* columnist Pendennis. 'He was wearing a stripey shirt.'

* * * * *

Chrystin Lyons, who lives next door to Viola Keats's old home, works in special effects at Pinewood Studios. Her latest film was *Batman Begins*. She said: 'I nearly ran Tom Cruise over in my jeep once. It was a very near miss.'

MAN ARGUS

* * * * *

Jodie Kidd is yet another victim of the volatile housing market. 'We've done up the house but can't sell it,' she said.

SUNDAY EXPRESS

* * * * *

Oprah Winfrey was turned away from one of the Paris boutiques of the luxury store Hermes after she and her entourage arrived 15 minutes after closing time. Oprah is said to have described it as one of the most humiliating experiences of her life.

DAILY EXPRESS

Mum-to-be Britney Spears had to cut short a romantic dinner out with husband Kevin Federline, after getting stomach cramps. Britney went home to rest and has recovered.

SUN

* * * * *

Cheryl Tweedy, a Newcastle pop singer, shopped for a birthday gift for her England footballer boyfriend, then changed her mind and had her right hand tattooed instead.

NORTHERN ECHO

FILM STAR KIRSTEN DUNST HAS WORN THE SAME SHOES TO EIGHT PARTIES IN TWO YEARS

DAILY STAR

NOT MANY DEAD

The *Northern Echo* reported that a woman named Michelle Bass, who has appeared on Channel 4's *Big Brother*, was not pregnant.

* * * * *

Kylie Minogue twisted her ankle while performing her new single for German TV. 'It was a nasty fall,' confirmed one onlooker.

DAILY TELEGRAPH

* * * * *

Bargain Hunters: Sandra Howard, wife of the Tory leader, bought a £75 dress from high-street store Monsoon for a winter ball.

DAILY MAIL

* * * * *

Dame Joan Plowright was spotted at 3.12 on Monday, shopping in Planet Organic on London's Westbourne Grove. Dame Joan's trolley contained some soya milk and a large watermelon.

GUARDIAN

Atomic Kitten star Natasha Hamilton, 21, has passed her driving test first time after a six-week intensive course.

DAILY MIRROR

David Furnish, long-term partner of Sir Elton John, needed help with his cuff-links when he stayed at the Feathers Hotel in Woodstock, Oxfordshire. The cuff-links were a gift from Sir Elton, but they were tricky to do up, so a member of staff helped him.

THE TIMES

Lord Hutton told me he had been putting his feet up since completing his infamous inquiry. 'I still go and sit on the Privy Council from time to time, but I'm retired now,' he told me. 'I'm finding it rather agreeable.'

EVENING STANDARD

NOT MANY DEAD

TV host Sharon Davies, 41, shocked fans with a bra-less outfit. The Beeb said, 'Not many people complained.'

Sexy fashion designer Sadie Frost returned home yesterday to find that she couldn't get in because she didn't have the right door key.

The designer Orla Kiely failed to watch an episode of *Diarmuid's Big Adventure* to which she had contributed. She explained: 'I was at home upstairs working on something while my husband was downstairs watching television. I assumed he was going to tell me when it was on, but he assumed that I was in the other room watching it.'

Fiona Bruce, the BBC *Ten O'Clock News* presenter, read the headlines last night assisted by a pair of glasses for the first time.

DAILY TELEGRAPH

* * * * *

David and Victoria Beckham have bought son Brooklyn three goldfish. They are named after his dad's football pals, Rio, Ronaldo and Figo.

GLOUCESTERSHIRE ECHO

* * * * *

For Kirsty Wark's birthday, her son James, aged 11, is cooking a five-course meal for the family.

THE TIMES

* * * * *

Michael Howard, canvassing for the European elections in Harrogate, helped his wife Sandra after she dropped her handbag, reported *The Times*, alongside two large photographs of Mr Howard bending down to pick up the bag, then standing up again.

NOT MANY DEAD

Getting back to nature on a fishing holiday in Iceland, the former Manchester United star Eric Cantona was woken by an earthquake measuring 5 on the Richter scale.

MAIL ON SUNDAY

* * * * *

'Maudie, our English setter, has died at the age of 10 and we miss her dreadfully,' says Anne Robinson on the front page of the *Daily Telegraph*.

* * * * *

He's renowned for his extravagant taste in ties and puns, but it's perhaps less well known that *Countdown* presenter Richard Whiteley's real first name is John. 'Yes, my full name is John Richard Whiteley,' the 59-year-old quiz show host confessed when we caught up with him.

RADIO TIMES

* * * * *

The actor Sir Alan Bates almost lost his footing while walking backwards from the Queen after being knighted.

THE TIMES

The Manchester United and England footballer Wayne Rooney's favourite food is lettuce, according to his fiancée.

DAILY TELEGRAPH

* * * * *

The son of Education Secretary Charles Clarke was suspended from school yesterday for swearing at a groundsman who confiscated his ball. Mr Clarke, the MP for Norwich South, said in a statement: 'My son was excluded for one day as a result of an incident where he swore at a member of the ground staff who confiscated his football.'

DAILY MAIL

* * * * *

A Welsh town has won the title of 'White Sock Capital of Britain' by buying more than 200 pairs a day from a local superstore. Celebrities famous for their white socks include Michael Jackson and Elvis Presley.

DAILY SPORT

BBC newsreader Anna Ford, 59, who is recovering from flu, had to give up halfway through yesterday's lunchtime bulletin because of a croaky voice.

GUARDIAN

The *Daily Telegraph* reports that supermodel Claudia Schiffer has given birth to a baby boy: 'The couple had been hoping for a natural birth, but Miss Schiffer was advised to have a Caesarean after she injured her foot.'

They were drinking VB bitter with all the locals, and at one point the quizmaster got Ricky to shout 'My arse' into his microphone.

THE DAILY TELEGRAPH COVERS RICKY
TOMLINSON'S HONEYMOON IN AUSTRALIA

Media magnate Rupert Murdoch may be worth £4 billion, but he still saves money by travelling on the subway when he is in New York.

DAILY MAIL

Titanic star Kate Winslet has been voted the healthiest-looking celebrity.

DAILY STAR

* * * * *

After They Were Famous (7.30 p.m.): This edition looks at Peter Wyngarde, who was a pin-up as Jason King but is now shaven-headed and enjoys clay-pigeon shooting.

KENT MESSENGER, 'WHAT'S ON'

* * * * *

Among the many people who last month recalled encounters with the late Sir John Gielgud was Mrs Elsie Harley, who once met him backstage at the Newcastle Theatre Royal.

She told the *Newcastle Journal*: 'I always remember Sir John's wonderful and distinctive voice asking, "Dry or sweet sherry, my dear?" "Dry, please," I answered. "My tipple, too," he said as he filled our glasses. We no longer breed stars like those.'

A poem etched on to a glass table made for Catherine Zeta Jones and Michael Douglas has a mistake in it. Their son is named after Dylan Thomas – whose poem 'In the Beginning' refers to 'ciphers' – but a slip has made it the meaningless 'cophers'. The Dylan Thomas Society said: 'They could always cover it up with a vase.'

DAILY MIRROR

* * * * *

Mariella Frostrup, a TV presenter, dropped into a Notting Hill health shop to buy a large coffee and two croissants.

DAILY MAIL

* * * * *

The *Daily Telegraph* offered insightful comment into Pete Townsend and Roger Daltrey's attendance at the funeral of The Who's bass player John Entwistle: 'Emerging from the funeral, neither said a word,' it reported.

The blue plaque honouring the life and work of Anna Freud – the psychoanalyst daughter of Sigmund – was unveiled for all of 15 minutes when John Cleese pulled the wrong cord and covered it up again.

DAILY TELEGRAPH

Richard Briers, the actor, was carrying an umbrella when he attended the premiere of *Stones in His Pockets* at the Duke of York's Theatre, reported the *Daily Express*. '"I thought the weather might turn inclement," he confided.'

Former President Bill Clinton has a new chocolate Labrador puppy, named Seamus, to replace his dog Buddy, who was killed by a car outside his New York home in Chappaqua in January. Seamus is Buddy's nephew and was born a month after Buddy died.

INDEPENDENT

The Pope had a surprise yesterday when a dove of peace released as he gave his weekly public greeting from a window overlooking St Peter's Square flew back inside his papal quarters. The Pope smiled as the dove was found fluttering round the room and re-released.

DAILY TELEGRAPH

* * * * *

EARL BURNS HAND COOKING STEAKS
'It's not serious, but it has caused him some discomfort,' says a spokesman.

DAILY TELEGRAPH

* * * * *

The *Sun* devoted half a page to the fact that the pop singer George Michael had been given a parking ticket for leaving his car on a double yellow line in Hampstead.

Reformed bachelor Gordon Brown is fully domesticated. From the wedding list of Toby Young, a friend of his brother-in-law, Gordon selected a casserole dish as his gift.

DAILY TELEGRAPH

* * * * *

Johnny Vaughan might be able to get out of bed in time to present *The Big Breakfast* every weekday – but he was late for Mass last Sunday. The 32-year-old TV star who hopes to be received into the Church at Easter was 15 minutes late for the 10 a.m. Mass at Holy Redeemer Church, Chelsea.

THE UNIVERSE

* * * * *

The *Daily Mail's* Nigel Dempster reported that when 'broadcasting goddess' Selina Scott flew to Majorca, a fellow passenger noticed that her hair was untidy at the back.

NOT MANY DEAD

Mark, the nine-week-old son of the film producer Henry Dent-Brocklehurst, wore ear defenders when he was taken by his mother Lilli to an air show at Rendcomb airfield, Cirencester, Glos., which included a display by the Red Arrows.

DAILY TELEGRAPH

* * * * *

Don't expect TV presenter Fern Britton to be going anywhere in a hurry – her two family cars are out of action.

DAILY MAIL

* * * * *

The New Zealand rugby player Jonah Lomu made a big impression when he went into the Three Kings pub for a drink, reported the *Richmond and Twickenham Times*. Customer Gareth Roberts said: 'We were just having some beers when someone said, "There's Jonah Lomu over there." Then we went back to drinking.'

John Hopkins reported in *The Times* that Oxford University rugby player Sam Adlen had played very well against Cambridge at Twickenham. He was born in Brynmawr, South Wales, explained Hopkins, where as a boy 'he was able to look out of the window of his parents' house and see opposite the house of the grandmother of J.P.R. Williams'.

* * * * *

Mel C, one of the Spice Girls, was seen buying pink Andrex lavatory paper in a local branch of Asda, according to the *Warrington Guardian.* Meanwhile the *News of the World* revealed that John Prescott had purchased groceries at a south London branch of Sainsbury's.

* * * * *

The *Daily Mail*'s Nigel Dempster spotted the novelist Anita Brookner 'standing imperiously outside the local Waitrose' in Chelsea at 8 a.m. one Saturday. 'Like me, she had thought the store opened at 8, not 8.30.'

NOT MANY DEAD

Passengers on a London to Leeds train 'watched fascinated' as playwright Alan Bennett ate 'homemade sandwiches wrapped in foil'.

DAILY MAIL

* * * * *

The Duke and Duchess of Hamilton have stopped shopping at the posh Edinburgh store Jenners because it sells pâté de foie gras.

DAILY TELEGRAPH

* * * * *

David Soul, the former star of the 1970s television series *Starsky and Hutch*, 'amazed' the owner of the Mace store at High Brooms near Tunbridge Wells by stopping to buy a loaf of bread, a pint of semi-skimmed milk and 20 Marlboro Lights cigarettes. 'He said he was staying in the area and he gave the impression he had just nipped out for a pint of milk,' said shopkeeper Nick Laing.

TUNBRIDGE WELLS COURIER

The worst thing about breaking her left shoulder, the singer Marianne Faithfull told the *Daily Telegraph*, was that she had had to use her right hand to smoke.

＊　＊　＊　＊　＊

Exiled Irish footballer Roy Keane is not the kind of chap to cross in a hurry. When the fiery midfielder faced the press outside his Cheshire home this week, one unfortunate reporter managed to tread on his beloved Labrador. It gave out a huge yelp of pain … Keane looked furious. Frankly the reporter was terrified and quickly hid behind colleagues.

DAILY TELEGRAPH

＊　＊　＊　＊　＊

I have done something that has changed my life and may change yours.

NIGELLA LAWSON IN THE TIMES ON HAVING LASER TREATMENT TO REMOVE HAIR FROM HER LEG

The former TUC chief Lord (Len) Murray is not being idle in retirement, we are informed by the *Times* Diary: 'The other day the peer, 77, was spotted washing up dirty coffee cups at the Methodist church in Loughton, Essex.'

✳ ✳ ✳ ✳ ✳

Television gardener Charlie Dimmock was among hundreds of commuters who had to wait for a delayed train to Hampshire at Waterloo station.

DAILY MAIL

✳ ✳ ✳ ✳ ✳

Jessica Callan of the *Daily Telegraph* has been confided in by Shuna Snow, daughter of the famous TV presenter Peter Snow. 'My father gets terribly affronted when people offer their seat to him on the bus,' she reveals.

DAILY MAIL

Television entertainer Ruby Wax wrote the landlord of a pub near Bath an IOU for £3.10 after finding herself short of cash to pay for her bar snacks.

WESTERN DAILY PRESS

✳ ✳ ✳ ✳ ✳

Darcey Bussell, the ballerina, often travels across London by Tube, rather than taking a chauffeur-driven car.

THE TIMES

✳ ✳ ✳ ✳ ✳

Nigel Reynolds of the *Daily Telegraph* reports an overheard conversation between Sir Peter Hall, wearing a fedora, and Michael Frayn. 'I've got a hat just like that,' Frayn told Sir Peter.

✳ ✳ ✳ ✳ ✳

Emilia Fox, actress daughter of Edward Fox, likes to revel in tales of blood-soiled diabolical murder. 'She is always reading something to do with crime,' a friend tells me.

DAILY TELEGRAPH

The *Evening Standard*'s Londoner's Diary reveals that at a book launch party the *Guardian* journalist Simon Hoggart spilled some wine on the shoes of Amanda Platell, William Hague's 'communications supremo'.

* * * * *

Chris Evans, a disc jockey, fell off his scooter when he was forced to brake suddenly on a wet road in 'London's trendy Notting Hill'. No one was hurt in the mishap.

DAILY MIRROR

* * * * *

The actress Patricia Hodge does not own a dog. However, she does have a wounded hedgehog, obtained from the RSPCA. 'It lives in our back garden where it looks after itself.'

THE TIMES

It is 'nail biting, always up-to-the-wire stuff', working for the BBC TV series *Ground Force*, presenter Alan Titchmarsh tells the *Radio Times*. For example, while filming recently the keys to the team's van became locked inside the vehicle. 'I have to admit I was getting angry,' says Titchmarsh. 'It held us up for an hour and a half.'

＊ ＊ ＊ ＊ ＊

The waste disposal machine in the kitchen of *Tatler* editor Geordie Greig has stopped working. Mr Greig has had to put his rubbish into plastic bin-liners instead.

DAILY TELEGRAPH

＊ ＊ ＊ ＊ ＊

John Saumarez Smith of the Heywood Hill bookshop in Mayfair has bought Enoch Powell's library. He tells us that Powell was a keen carpenter, and the house is full of shelves he made himself and put in ingenious places for his ever-growing collection.

THE TIMES

NOT MANY DEAD

Mrs Damien Hirst (wife of the artist Damien Hirst) came third in a surfing competition in Biarritz.

DAILY TELEGRAPH

* * * * *

Elle Macpherson, the model, was sauntering down Kensington High Street in ballerina slippers and a frilly skirt when it bucketed down. A taxi eventually stopped, but declared her too bedraggled, leaving the poor girl to walk.

THE TIMES

* * * * *

The Rochdale bus-stop shooting happened outside the home of pop star Lisa Stanfield's mother-in-law, who was working out at a local gymnasium when the attack happened.

THE TIMES

The comedian Eddie Izzard's favourite film is *The Great Escape*. 'It has a very complex plot,' he told the *Daily Telegraph*'s 'Peterborough' column.

* * * * *

Wayne Rooney's fiancée Coleen McLoughlin carried her dog in Cheshire. Both wore hooded tops.

DAILY EXPRESS

ROYAL REVELATIONS

ONE OF THE QUEEN'S RACING PIGEONS HAS GONE MISSING

DAILY EXPRESS

Earl Spencer, brother of the late Princess of Wales, loves books. But his appetite for reading has taken its toll on his eyes and he has now been prescribed glasses for reading.

SUNDAY EXPRESS

* * * *

Royal bride-to-be Sophie Rhys-Jones took a train trip alone – second class. Sophie, 34, bought a £19 return ticket from London to Liverpool – instead of the £155 first-class fare.

SUN

NOT MANY DEAD

Dino the corgi yawns as he waits for the Queen and Prince Philip to tour a shopping centre in Potsdam, south of Berlin, yesterday, as part of a state visit to Germany.

CAPTION IN THE OXFORD MAIL ACCOMPANYING A PICTURE OF A CORGI YAWNING

✳ ✳ ✳ ✳ ✳

The *Westmorland Gazette* reported that on a recent visit to the Lake District Prince William opened the door to a newspaper shop for two friends who wanted to buy lottery tickets.

✳ ✳ ✳ ✳ ✳

The Countess of Wessex returned from St Moritz in Switzerland on crutches after pulling a calf muscle while skiing.

DAILY TELEGRAPH

✳ ✳ ✳ ✳ ✳

Camilla Parker Bowles ran to catch up with the Prince of Wales after attending church with him at Sandringham. She was holding a bunch of red tulips.

THE TIMES

The organisers of the Olympic Games in Sydney apologised to the Princess Royal after an official accidentally touched her elbow. The Princess had not noticed the contact, but received an apology anyway because it was a 'breach of protocol'.

DAILY TELEGRAPH

✳ ✳ ✳ ✳ ✳

The Duke of Kent yesterday nipped into his local Safeway supermarket in West London to pick up a few essentials. Dressed in a green cord blazer, chinos and trainers, the Duke, 67, who is a grandmaster of the Freemasons and president of the All England Tennis Club, bought an 83p box of Bisto gravy and a packet of Smints.

DAILY MAIL

Prince William was among the audience for a matinée showing of *Lord of the Rings: Return of the King*. The Prince's party bought five Cornetto ice-creams – three strawberry-flavoured and two mint – during the interval.

LANCASHIRE EVENING TELEGRAPH

✳ ✳ ✳ ✳ ✳

A *Sun* 'Royal Special' reported that the Queen had downed a glass of sparkling wine 'in one'.

✳ ✳ ✳ ✳ ✳

The Earl and Countess of Wessex sent their chauffeur out to buy fish and chips when they discovered the chef of a Scottish palace was having the night off. Edward and Sophie enjoyed two £4.50 portions of haddock and chips from Bene chip shop on Edinburgh's Royal Mile, 300 yards from Holyroodhouse, where they were staying.

DAILY MAIL

The Duke of Kent's son, Lord Nicholas Windsor, has 'forfeited the royal line' in order to become a Roman Catholic. He was 25th in line to the throne.

DAILY TELEGRAPH

* * * * *

Former royal press 'minder' Dickie Arbiter could earn £250,000 by cashing in on his fund of stories about the Queen and her family, reported the *Sunday Times*. The paper gave an example: Arbiter once helped clear up after an informal picnic at Balmoral. He said to the Queen, 'I'll wash, you dry?' but she replied, 'No, I'll wash, you dry.'

* * * * *

The Princess Royal's children, Peter and Zara Phillips, attended the Gatcombe horse trials on their mother's estate in the Cotswolds, reported the *Daily Express*. Peter and Zara 'laughed uproariously' as they 'swapped jokes', wrote Michael Paterson. 'At one point Peter lounged on the grass with a dog.'

NOT
MANY
DEAD

Nigel Dempster reported in the *Daily Mail* that Anthony Julius, the solicitor who arranged the late Princess of Wales's divorce, 'did not drive straight home after shopping at Tesco's flagship supermarket on the North Circular at Friern Barnet'. Instead, he took his children to a nearby adventure playground.

* * * * *

Prince Charles met Rita Marley, widow of the late reggae star Bob Marley, during his recent visit to Trench Town, Jamaica. 'Mrs Marley was ecstatic to see the Prince in a place which held so many happy memories for her,' reported the *Daily Telegraph*. '"I first had sex with Bob in this community centre," she explained.'

Prince William's former nanny, Tiggy Legge-Bourke, had her hen-night one Tuesday in October, 'the *Mail on Sunday* can reveal'.

＊ ＊ ＊ ＊ ＊

The Prince of Wales met the pop star Prince at a charity gala dinner. 'The two princes enjoyed a five-minute conversation, with Prince Charles asking the singer if he had a special place where he composed his music. The singer smiled and said, "Yes."'

DAILY TELEGRAPH

PROVINCIAL PANDEMONIUM

WOMAN, 79, HAS TO CUT VERGES

SOMERSET COUNTY GAZETTE

A police inquiry has begun following reports that a man kicked a duck at Saumarez Park in Guernsey.

CEEFAX

* * * * *

A cycling flasher exposed himself to a woman in Cambridge … police have not issued a description of the man apart from the fact that he was on a bike.

CAMBRIDGE EVENING NEWS

The new chief executive of Scarborough Council has been taken ill, three weeks after taking over the top post at the local authority. Jim Dillon has been off work for a couple of days after being laid low with a heavy cold.

SCARBOROUGH EVENING NEWS

✻ ✻ ✻ ✻ ✻

A Cadbury's Creme Egg was thrown through a window at Hurstleigh Terrace.

HARROGATE ADVERTISER

✻ ✻ ✻ ✻ ✻

Because of the lack of fish supplies, no fish vans have called locally in Oban for weeks. But on Tuesday 29th November one van arrived in Scalpayl with fresh supplies of various species of fish.

OBAN TIMES

✻ ✻ ✻ ✻ ✻

In an interview with the local Black Cat bookshop, the *Leicester Mercury* asked, 'What's your best customer story?' 'Someone asked for books about horses by Francis Dickinson. He meant Dick Francis.'

The letter 'e' has mysteriously vanished from the side of the Tesco Express store in Thornwell. Someone, who wished to remain nameless, said, 'To be honest, I hadn't even noticed it had gone missing.'

MONMOUTHSHIRE FREE PRESS

* * * * *

A flowerpot was damaged in Wind Street, Llandsyul, at around 7.30 p.m. on Saturday November 26th.

TIVY-SIDE ADVERTISER

* * * * *

A 45-minute discussion between parish councillors resulted in the decision that each item on the agenda should take ten minutes.

BURTON MAIL

* * * * *

An egg was thrown at a home in Strawberry Field, Pulborough, at 7.30 p.m. on Monday October 31st, Hallowe'en night, reported police.

WEST SUSSEX COUNTY TIMES

The Fire Brigade rescued a trapped seagull from Victoria Avenue on Monday lunchtime. The seagull's injuries were not life-threatening.

HASTINGS AND ST LEONARD'S OBSERVER

* * * * *

Musician Dr Zeus did not perform with bhangra group RDB at the Sun-Kissed Asian flavas concert, held in Valentines Park on Sunday.

ILFORD RECORDER

* * * * *

Four Forest Health councillors mingled with royalty when they attended a garden party at Buckingham Palace.

NEWMARKET JOURNAL

COUNCIL TO MAKE RUBBISH DECISION

BELPER NEWS

A thief entered the conservatory of a home on Prince Edward's Road, Lewes, early on Sunday morning and stole a wooden box which contained nothing of any value. It was later found on the doorstep of a neighbouring house.

SUSSEX EXPRESS

* * * * *

The high number of bicycles stolen in Oxford is due to the high number of students who find cycling the easiest way to get around.

OXFORD TIMES

* * * * *

Police are looking for 30,000 bees missing from a hive in Pershore, Worcs. 'They could have travelled in any direction,' said a spokesman.

[SOURCE UNKNOWN]

* * * * *

The splendid new curtains which have now been erected in Tavistock Town Hall were declared a great success by members of the town council's properties committee at their meeting last week.

TAVISTOCK TIMES

A garage on Silk Mill Road, Watford, was broken into. No property was stolen, only moved about in the garage.

WATFORD ADVERTISER

* * * *

Thanks to successful engineering works, non-stopping trains will now pass through Burton at 50mph instead of 30mph.

BURTON ADVERTISER

* * * *

A full can of lager was lobbed over a security gate at Park Lane in Saffron Walden and hit a tiled roof at around 12.30 a.m. on Wednesday last week.

SAFFRON WALDEN OBSERVER

* * * *

Police received reports that salad cream had been smeared on the windows of the parish council at Bouverie Hall at the weekend.

MARLBOROUGH-PEWSEY GAZETTE AND HERALD

Travellers camping illegally in the south of Northamptonshire stay for a shorter time than anywhere else in the country.

* * * * *

A Bridgnorth worker was reading an email from a friend of hers who was holidaying in Australia. Perplexed by some of the comments relating to a dog – she did not have one – and putting money in the bank – no such bank – she read further. It emerged that her friend had accidentally sent an email intended for her father.

FED UP DINNER LADY QUITS

LOUGHBOROUGH ECHO

NOT MANY DEAD

A security guard on patrol at a building site in Liversedge last week returned to his office to find thieves had stolen two packets of peanuts. 'Police believe that one packet was salted and the other dry-roasted.'

DEWSBURY PRESS

* * * * *

An overhead extractor fan caused smoke to rise from the ladies' toilets in the Coach Street car park, Skipton. The incident was reported at 9.20 a.m. on Saturday.

CRAVEN HERALD

* * * * *

A woman whooped with joy when a planning application for a house in Clay Hills, Pebmarsh, was approved by Braintree councillors.

HALSTEAD GAZETTE

* * * * *

Four pints of milk valued at £1.76 have been stolen from the front of a house in Julian Road, Ludlow.

LUDLOW ADVERTISER

Tyre and exhaust fitters in Crowborough have welcomed the news that out of 20 different professions, car mechanics and tyre technicians were the eighth happiest in their jobs.

KENT AND SUSSEX COURIER

❋ ❋ ❋ ❋ ❋

At about 8 p.m. on 10th February an unknown person reached into the broken lens of a Ford Mondeo's indicator and stole the bulb. The estimated value of the stolen property is £1.

BELPER NEWS

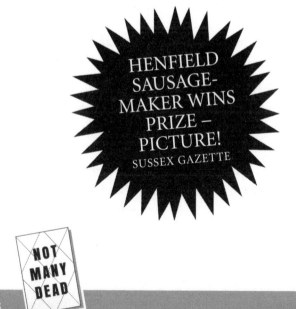

HENFIELD SAUSAGE-MAKER WINS PRIZE – PICTURE!

SUSSEX GAZETTE

NOT MANY DEAD

For the second month running, Hunston Parish council chairman Ray Harle has had to report failure in his hunt for a suitable air freshener to take the pong out of the council meetings at Hunston Village Hall.

CHICHESTER OBSERVER

* * * * *

A wing mirror was ripped off the driver's-side door of a Rover 25 parked on Auckland Way, Whitby, overnight.

WHITBY GAZETTE

* * * * *

A random survey of Wells pubs produced the same verdict everywhere. There is a run on ice-cold lager.

WELLS JOURNAL AT THE HEIGHT OF A HEAT-WAVE

* * * * *

Residents complained to police at the weekend after a man was seen loitering outside Denby Pottery. It turned out he had been conducting a traffic census.

[SOURCE UNKNOWN]

Mystery surrounds a piglet found wandering in Ravensthorpe. It was found in Huddersfield Road yesterday and taken to Dewsbury police station. RSPCA inspector Dave Holgate said: 'How this piglet came to be wandering the streets is a complete mystery.'

HUDDERSFIELD EXAMINER

* * * * *

A thief started the New Year on the wrong foot, reported the *Suffolk Mercury*, when he stole a bin containing 27 right-footed slippers from outside a Sudbury shoe shop. Store manager Hayley Chatters said: 'Nothing like this has ever happened before and we are all gobsmacked.' A police spokesman added: 'This was a very unfortunate incident, because the crime rate in Sudbury was very low over the Christmas period.'

* * * * *

A windscreen wiper on a Skoda in Chapel Road, Brightlingsea, has been bent.

FRINTON AND WALTON ADVERTISER

NOT MANY DEAD

Glossop Police were called to Manor Park on Friday night. A resident found an injured duck and also called an RSPCA officer. The duck was taken to Victoria Vets at 9 p.m. but died at 9.30 p.m. with the policeman present.

GLOSSOP CHRONICLE

* * * * *

Thieves stole a tray of baked beans and a box of washing tablets from a garage in Brunswick Street, Leamington, between Sunday at noon and Wednesday.

LEAMINGTON SPA COURIER

* * * * *

A group of cows freed themselves from a field in Lower Kilburn last week.

BELPER NEWS

* * * * *

A Loughborough pensioner has given 'a big thank you' to Charnwood Borough council for their prompt action in putting a new lock on her front door. The woman, who asked not to be named, also thanked Lifeline for their help in passing on the message and the workman for doing the job.

LOUGHBOROUGH ECHO

A white plastic number '1' was stolen from Unit 17, Glanyrafon Fawr, overnight on Friday 5th July.

CUMBRIAN NEWS

* * * * *

Salford chief executive Dave Tarry was spotted with a big bag of toffees at the start of the match at Halifax. He passed them down the line to chairman John Wilkinson and his wife and other Reds officials.

MANCHESTER EVENING NEWS

* * * * *

A coffee morning at the Church House this Saturday will be held in the aid of the Mid Wales Breathing Club.

WELSHPOOL DISTRICT NEWS

* * * * *

The *Northern Echo* reported that Sue Sweeney, a local radio DJ who failed in an ITV contest to win a role in the soap *Emmerdale*, complained: 'The decision was utter hell. I am still afraid of going out shopping, because people comment about what happened.'

WORKER, 58, CUTS FINGER

EAST GRINSTEAD COURIER

There were furtive glances at Cardigan Courthouse when local solicitor Peter Wiggan was seen carrying a large black lady's handbag. It turned out that having completed his business Mr Wiggan had noticed that colleague Mary Lewis-Symmonds had left her handbag on the solicitors' table, and the chivalrous lawyer returned it to her.

TIVY-SIDE ADVERTISER

* * * * *

A front-page story with picture in the *Ham and High* tells how former nurse 87-year-old Hettie Collier failed to speak to Tony Blair when he visited a local hospital.

An Aberdeen man has been reunited with his wife's shopping basket after losing it in a car park more than a week ago.

ABERDEEN PRESS AND JOURNAL

Staff at Torquay's Riviera Centre are to repair a window which cracked when a seagull flew into it.

HERALD EXPRESS

Members of the Brookland and District Gardeners' Society were disappointed last Wednesday when the speaker, Gary McArthur, failed to turn up. Instead, members cleaned the cupboard in the village hall, and then discussed forthcoming outings.

KENTISH EXPRESS

Penguins at Marwell Zoo near Winchester 'looked up in astonishment' when it snowed at the end of December.

DAILY MAIL

The Revd David Wood, vicar of All Saints Church, Bolton, near Appleby, arrived at a coffee morning in the town by bicycle.

CUMBERLAND AND WESTMORLAND HERALD

'Great changes' at Hartfield parish council meetings: coffee will be served in future 'with parish clerk Louise supervising the operation'.

EAST SUSSEX COURIER

* * * * *

Sandiacre parish councillors heard that groups of youngsters congregating near St Giles church had been moved on by police and were now gathering near a school in Victoria Road. 'No reports of damage have been received,' said the *Ilkeston Advertiser*. 'The youngsters were polite to a caretaker at the school when asked to move.'

* * * * *

A puzzled Foxhill resident contacted police to say he had found a pair of shoes dumped in his garden.

BEXHILL OBSERVER

PC Woods of Dorking Police is investigating a fire in a toilet roll in the men's lavatory in St Martin's Walk. 'During the incident the toilet sustained smoke damage, especially to the roll holder.'

DORKING ADVERTISER

Thirty passengers on one of Travel Dundee's new 'eco-friendly' coaches were locked on board for 10 minutes while the driver went to consult a manual because he didn't know how to switch the lights on.

THE TIMES

Residents and shopkeepers in Uckfield, East Sussex, are not opposing plans for a new McDonald's hamburger restaurant. Most think that it will be good for trade, that it will appeal to young people, and that the town will be able to cope with any extra traffic.

INDEPENDENT ON SUNDAY

DISASTER LOOMS

LUCKY ESCAPE AS CAR JUST MISSES WOMAN

NEWMARKET WEEKLY NEWS

England football team manager Sven-Göran Eriksson's house in Regent's Park was broken into on Monday, but nothing was taken.

CAMDEN JOURNAL

* * * * *

Thirty middle-aged people went to a summer solstice rave in a field by the Thanet Way, near the Roman Galley on Saturday night. A public order officer told them to leave by 9 a.m. on Sunday, which they did.

ISLE OF THANET GAZETTE

NOT MANY DEAD

Reports of a dead boy on Jacksons Lane in Belper were made to police on Monday afternoon. But when officers arrived at the scene they discovered the body was a girl who was lying down because she was tired.

BELPER NEWS

* * * * *

A dog got its head stuck fast in a gate in Immingham on Wednesday. Firefighters from Immingham East fire station were called to help the animal in Margaret Street at 3.56 p.m. However, when they arrived they found the dog had released itself and walked away.

GRIMSBY TELEGRAPH

* * * * *

A police car sped to the centre of Wells on Friday afternoon after information that there was an incident and shouting was heard. But police found no trace of anyone.

WELLS JOURNAL

* * * * *

A housewife who reported all the washing stolen from her line to the police at East Grinstead phoned later to say she'd found it.

EAST GRINSTEAD COURIER

Brilliant Brookborough scientist, Anita Kirkpatrick, missed being caught up in last Saturday's horrific car bomb massacre in Bali by days. She had left Indonesia a week before.

JOHANNESBURG STAR

✳ ✳ ✳ ✳ ✳

A spot check on a school bus at Ysgol Gyfun Llangefni revealed only a few minor defects that were rectified on site.

WESTERN DAILY MAIL

AIRGUN PELLET NEARLY STRIKES CHILD'S HEAD

BROMLEY AND HAYES NEWS SHOPPER

NOT MANY DEAD

When filming, Martin Cole struck his co-star Tamzin Outhwaite a little too hard with a pistol. He thought he had ruined her face, but in fact there was no skin broken.

DAILY MAIL

* * * * *

Two empty passenger trains travelling towards each other on the same line came to a halt 100 yards apart. Connex said safety measures stopped them colliding.

THE TIMES

* * * * *

The *Tivyside Advertiser* reports a close shave concerning the Mayor's Ball, to be held on 13th April next year:

When Mayor Cllr John Adams-Lewis announced that at last week's meeting of the town council, Cllr Llwyd Edwards asked, 'Is that a Friday?' The Mayor replied: 'No, everything is all right, it's a Saturday.'

A royal protection officer guarding Prince William dropped his gun as the prince left a West End restaurant. It did not go off and there was no risk to any individual.

DAILY TELEGRAPH

＊ ＊ ＊ ＊ ＊

Television presenter Zoe Ball and her pop star husband Norman Cook were almost involved in an accident on the M23 near Gatwick. Mr Cook, also known as 'Fatboy Slim', was driving the couple's Mercedes when a car in front skidded on the wet road 'causing him to brake hard'.

SURREY MIRROR

＊ ＊ ＊ ＊ ＊

Police who went to round up some straying sheep in Derbyshire found that the animals had already returned to their field.

MATLOCK MERCURY

An unnamed lady cyclist was not badly hurt when she fell off her bike in Burgess Hill.

BRIGHTON ARGUS

* * * * *

A sea-search launched after two divers failed to surface off Portland Bill was called off after they surfaced.

DORSET ECHO

* * * * *

Whitby firefighters were not called into action when heavy rain caused floods in some areas.

WHITBY GAZETTE

* * * * *

The *Yorkshire Post* reports that when Richard Whiteley arrived late in London recently for his Channel 4 game show *Countdown*, he had to ride pillion on a motorcycle supplied by the TV company in order to get to the studio on time. 'My heart was in my mouth,' he said.

RSPCA officers, alerted when a neighbour saw Jet, an Alsatian, mauling what she thought was its Gloucestershire owner's rabbit, found the pet safe in its run. The victim turned out to be a slipper.

THE TIMES

Irish actor James Nesbitt almost knocked over a cyclist after a few too many beers … luckily the cyclist spotted him and managed to swerve out of the way.

DAILY SKETCH

ARE OUR SCHOOLS SAFE?
A random Herald survey suggests yes.
CALGARY HERALD

NOT MANY DEAD

Police are still on the lookout for coloured lights that are fitted to vehicles. There were no reports of that nature last week.

ST HELENA HERALD

* * * * *

Firefighters from Shrewsbury were called to a house after a pigeon became entangled in a TV roof aerial … by the time the engine arrived it had freed itself.

SHREWSBURY CHRONICLE

* * * * *

A car in a convoy taking International Development Minister Clare Short on a visit to Pontinak in Borneo overturned in West Kalimantan province, reported the *Glasgow Herald*. Ms Short was not hurt. She was not in the car.

Thieves failed to break into a garden shed at the back of a home in Stewart Street, Barrow Island, between 5.30 a.m. and 9 a.m. yesterday.

NORTH WEST EVENING MAIL

* * * * *

King Carl Gustaf XVI of Sweden ran into the back of a car with his BMW but neither driver was hurt.

THE TIMES

PROOF
AT LAST

SCIENTISTS PROVE WEARING BLACK MAKES YOU LOOK SLIMMER

DAILY EXPRESS

People who walk dogs walk more than those who don't walk dogs.

AMERICAN JOURNAL OF PREVENTATIVE MEDICINE

* * * * *

A study of the electricity consumed by electrical devices shows that people could save money by switching them off.

BBC WEBSITE

* * * * *

A healthy lifestyle can give elderly people a better chance of living longer.

WESTERN MAIL

73 per cent of people said that offices would be more pleasant if people made an effort to be nicer.

METRO

* * * * *

World population is falling. The US Census Bureau partly attributes the drop to women having fewer babies.

BBC CEEFAX

* * * * *

Britons are the second most embarrassed in Europe over their passport picture; they spend, on average, just 10 minutes having their picture taken.

DAILY TELEGRAPH

* * * * *

Nearly one third of Britons who have an electric drill, saw or other power tool haven't plugged it in during the past year.

ABBEY NATIONAL SURVEY

RESEARCHER LINKS OBESITY TO LARGE FOOD PORTIONS

DAVAO SUN & STAR, PHILIPPINES

ITV newscaster Trevor McDonald is the nation's most trusted figure, with 43 per cent of those polled claiming to trust him 'a great deal', followed by Channel 5's Kirsty Young at 24 per cent … said a report into television news.

WESTERN DAILY PRESS

✳ ✳ ✳ ✳ ✳

Workers really don't like Mondays, according to a study by Mark Taylor of Essex University.

GUARDIAN

✳ ✳ ✳ ✳ ✳

Shoppers in Diss, Norfolk, buy more Brussels sprouts than anywhere else in Britain.

THE TIMES

NOT MANY DEAD

The lounge is our favourite room.

* * * * *

Politics has become a taboo subject at the dinner table.

* * * * *

Britain has been dubbed the 'Don't know' capital of the European Union following a survey about its work. Even basic questions got more 'Don't know's than in any other state.

* * * * *

Night-clubbers who ditch spectacles in favour of contact lenses can increase their 'pulling-power' by up to 400 per cent, university researchers have found. The research was carried out on 38 volunteers.

* * * * *

Most Britons aged between 18 and 25 intend to get drunk on New Year's Eve.

In response to a survey which revealed that 'many people watch TV advertisements with the sound off', a spokesperson for the London Business School remarked: 'This could send shockwaves through the industry.'

❋ ❋ ❋ ❋ ❋

New research says that if more of us spent our lunchtimes relaxing in a park we would return to work refreshed, with renewed energy levels and enthusiasm.

BRISTOL EVENING POST

CATS LOVE
PEOPLE
WHO LOVE
CATS
GUARDIAN

SELF-SERVING SURVEYS

Being careful with your cash is sexy. A recent survey had shown that more than half of Britons thought being able to manage money makes you more attractive to the opposite sex.

SURVEY COMMISSIONED BY THE HALIFAX

* * * * *

The Tameside Citizens Panel Newsletter conducted a survey about its crematoria and found that: 'the main reason for visiting a cemetery/crematorium is to attend a funeral or visit a grave'.

* * * * *

British women are spending an increasing amount of time worrying about cleaning.

SURVEY COMMISSIONED BY MOLLY MAID, A
CONTRACT CLEANING FRANCHISE

Eight out of ten Britons feared becoming victims of identity thieves who sift through people's rubbish to glean personal information.

SURVEY COMMISSIONED BY FELLOWES, MANUFACTURERS OF PAPER SHREDDERS

＊ ＊ ＊ ＊ ＊

Mums are feeling the strain, with 91 per cent saying they feel under pressure to be perfect. They blame the media, schools and the Government.

SURVEY CARRIED OUT BY A CONTRACEPTIVE FIRM

＊ ＊ ＊ ＊ ＊

'Cheese does not give you nightmares,' reveals a survey by the Cheese Council. 'We hope we have at last debunked the myth,' said a Cheese Council spokesman. However their survey did reveal that 75 per cent of men and 85 per cent of women said that after eating Stilton, they experienced 'odd and vivid dreams'.

Fewer than one in five Britons wants a 'New York-style' smoking ban in public places.

SURVEY CARRIED OUT BY TOBACCO COMPANIES

✳ ✳ ✳ ✳ ✳

White Van Man is not really rude; his behaviour is caused by stress and frustration.

SURVEY OF 200 COMMERCIAL DRIVERS –
BY COMMERCIAL FLEET MANAGEMENT
COMPANY RYDER

✳ ✳ ✳ ✳ ✳

Voluntary workers are less likely to suffer from stress and depression, according to a survey.

SURVEY COMMISSIONED BY COMMUNITY
SERVICE VOLUNTEERS

A breakfast of beans on toast helps keeps schoolgirls top of the class

SURVEY PART-FUNDED BY HEINZ

NOT MANY DEAD

More than £351 million-worth of DVDs are piling up bought but unwatched on people's shelves.

SURVEY BY SCREENSELECT.CO.UK,
A DVD RENTAL COMPANY

✳ ✳ ✳ ✳ ✳

Most graduates feel their degrees are useless and almost three out of ten are bored with their jobs. Almost half of those aged 35 and under said they were not being intellectually challenged. One in five said they were disillusioned and 27 per cent said they were contemplating a career switch.

SURVEY CARRIED OUT BY
THE TEACHER TRAINING AGENCY

✳ ✳ ✳ ✳ ✳

Women are at their happiest when they ditch their boyfriends and go out for a drink and a chinwag with girlfriends.

SURVEY FOR THE MAKERS OF BLISS,
A NEW DRINK AIMED AT WOMEN

Women who spend the most time doing household chores have the highest sex drive.

SURVEY COMMISSIONED BY MINKY,
A MANUFACTURER OF DOMESTIC APPLIANCES

* * * * *

Andrex Moist toilet tissue has carried out a survey in Wales and the West to find out just how confident we really are. The shocking results reveal 88 per cent of us are letting lack of confidence prevent us doing the things we really want to do. And the one thing that 69 per cent of people cited as most affecting their confidence? Not feeling 100 per cent fresh and clean.

BATH CHRONICLE

* * * * *

People nowadays would rather be sacked by video-conference than 'almost any other method'.

SURVEY CARRIED OUT BY MASERGY,
A VIDEO-CONFERENCING SPECIALIST

(In fact, what the survey actually revealed was that people would much prefer to be sacked in person. They only preferred a video-conference firing to being given the boot by phone or post.)

NOT
MANY
DEAD

David Lewis, a media psychologist, has found in trials that people drinking more than two and a half glasses of water a day are four times less likely to catch a cold or flu than those drinking less.

SURVEY SPONSORED BY A
WATER FILTER MANUFACTURER

* * * * *

The healthiest people in the West are those who own dogs and regularly take them for walks.

SURVEY COMMISSIONED BY PETPLAN INSURANCE

* * * * *

Britons have up to £100 million in loose change lying around the house: hidden in corners, behind furniture and under sofa cushions.

SURVEY COMMISSIONED BY MOLLY MAID,
THE CONTRACT CLEANING FRANCHISE

* * * * *

65 per cent of National Lottery millionaires are happier now that they have won the Lottery.

SURVEY COMMISSIONED BY
THE NATIONAL LOTTERY

Almost one-fifth of Devon women would prefer to cut their toenails than clean the house.

SURVEY COMMISSIONED BY VILEDA, MAKERS OF THE 'SUPERMOP' AND OTHER CLEANING PRODUCTS

* * * * *

Four out of ten employers would gladly take a pay cut for a new job that was more rewarding in other ways ... the research was commissioned to raise awareness of social work.

EXETER EXPRESS & ECHO

* * * * *

Nearly two-thirds of homeowners would rather improve their homes than move.

SURVEY CARRIED OUT BY DIY GROUP FOCUS WICKES

BELGIAN WINS NEAR-RECORD SUM IN LOTTERY

REUTERS

NOT MANY DEAD

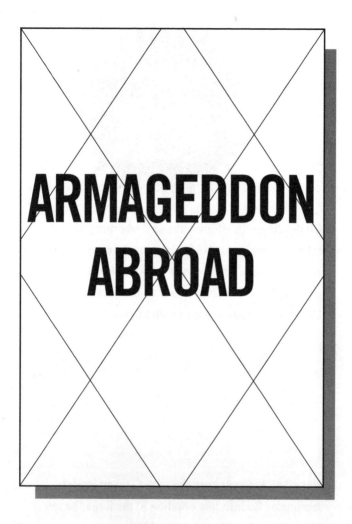

ARMAGEDDON
ABROAD

MAN FALLS FROM COCONUT TREE, HURT
DAVAO SUN STAR, PHILIPPINES

Gladys Reyes [a Filipina actress] has three dining tables. There is a table for important occasions and special guests. Another one is for the kitchen and everyday use. The third one is in the garage which Chris [her husband] uses when he has visitors.

PHILIPPINES SUN & STAR

✳ ✳ ✳ ✳ ✳

Volcano eruption in Mexico leaves no victims.

EL PAIS

✳ ✳ ✳ ✳ ✳

Hannibal, the youngest son of the Libyan leader, Muammar Gadafy, has enrolled at the Copenhagen Business School to pursue an MBA.

GUARDIAN

NOT MANY DEAD

No Canadians make Booker shortlist.

CANADIAN CANWEST NEWS SERVICE

* * * * *

Every day outside a Northbridge eatery a postie pokes the mail, one item at a time, through a thin crack under the doors. The Fishy Affair doesn't have a slot or a postbox.

WESTERN AUSTRALIA SUNDAY TIMES

* * * * *

Los Angeles Lakers superstar center Shaquille O'Neal will skip this weekend's all-star game to rest his arthritic right big toe.

PHILIPPINES SUN & STAR

* * * * *

Lech Walesa, the symbol of resistance to Communist rule and former president of Poland, has shaved off his moustache.

DAILY TELEGRAPH

* * * * *

Avocado lovers warned over knife accidents.

NEW ZEALAND SUNDAY STAR-TIMES

A surfer bitten in the side by a shark off Australia's East Coast said he would not have been able to swim for safety if it had bitten his arm off.

SUNDAY TELEGRAPH

* * * * *

Quiet vote is held in Macedonia.

INTERNATIONAL HERALD TRIBUNE

* * * * *

Nigel Dempster reports in the *Daily Mail* that, although they are forbidden on British racecourses, dogs are 'a welcome addition' at Baden-Baden races. On a recent visit he revealed that he had seen two pointers, a retriever, a poodle, a Jack Russell, two greyhounds and a long-haired dachshund.

* * * * *

The German chancellor, Gerhard Schroeder, visited the Fraunhofer Institute, a microchip technology laboratory in the north German town of Itzehoe, reported the *Daily Telegraph*, where he met the prime minister of Schleswig Holstein, Heide Simonis.

AND FINALLY

West Country has bendiest road.

THE TIMES

* * * * *

Unknown leads a squad of unknowns.

CRICKET LINE-UP NEWS FROM CRICINFO.COM

* * * * *

Sally Paxman, 37, of Whitton, said she had become more interested in cricket recently. 'I don't understand it really. My husband explained it to me when it was on.'

RICHMOND INFORMER

* * * * *

Offender tuned into Radio 4 in prison and got hooked on *The Archers*.

GUARDIAN WEEKLY

NOT
MANY
DEAD

It is extraordinary to reflect that, had Tony Blair not decided to take a year off between leaving Fettes and going up to Oxford, he might have run into the 14-year-old Osama Bin Laden amid the dreaming spires.

SUNDAY TELEGRAPH

MUSICIANS UNITED BY LOVE OF MUSIC

MANCHESTER METRO NEWS

NOT
MANY
DEAD